LEARNING TO WALK AGAIN

Penny McIntyre-Crain

DORRANCE
PUBLISHING CO
EST. 1920
PITTSBURGH, PENNSYLVANIA 15238

Dorrance Publishing Co
585 Alpha Drive
Suite 103
Pittsburgh, PA 15238
Visit our website at *www.dorrancebookstore.com*

ISBN: 979-8-88729-372-1
eISBN: 979-8-88729-872-6

It is my honor, which is so full of gratitude,
To dedicate this book to my two treasured sisters,
Darlene McEntire and Pamela Crain

ACKNOWLEDGMENTS

I must also acknowledge my friend,
Heidi Parton Odom
for her unshakable friendship
during some of the hardest times in my life.

Lastly, I must acknowledge my two beautiful daughters,
Mary Elizabeth (Moore-Butler) Wright
and
Taylor Kathleen Butler
They have inspired me since the day they were born and
continue to encourage me to better every day.

PREFACE

As babies, we come into this world with certain goals set for us by design and by our parents. We are expected to cry when we leave the womb, and if we do not, the doctor will do what he or she must to ensure we clear our lungs. We move from crying to sucking, whether on the breast or the bottle…so we learn to eat. We grow quickly and learn to acknowledge faces… we smile, we laugh, and again cry depending on what we are wanting to achieve. Through observation of our parents, we learn to make noises, i.e., learn to talk. We later realize that movement is a necessary means to get what we want, so we learn to scoot, crawl, pull-up, and finally…**we learn to walk**.

As we realize our freedom through movement, we begin to explore our surroundings. We are not afraid because, up to this point, we know we can rely on our parents to protect us. We know they will catch us if we fall. We learn to trust. We learn to love. We learn to hope, to dream, and to have faith that we are on this earth for a purpose. We may not know what that is for some time, but we know life is good, people are good, our parents are good; and depending on how we are raised…we learn God is good.

We grow and learn through the institutions we are exposed to… such as faith-based institutions, grade school, high school, and eventually college. Again, we know that there is a purpose for our life and because of the encouragement and teaching we have received, we have no doubt we can do what we must to achieve our goals. Even when we stumble and fall, we know there is someone who loves us and will always be there to pick us up and protect us. Life is Good!

It's a lovely story…a life without pitfalls, a life with the perfect family that supports and protects throughout your life. The family that says, "I will be there when you need me. I will protect you through the darkness and rejoice with you in the light. You are safe, so…proceed on because darkness is simply the absence of light and nothing more."

If you are reading this, you know that is simply a lovely story and darkness can be so much more than the absence of light. It is loss… the loss of trust, the loss of faith in humanity…the loss of faith. It is mourning…the mourning of all you thought was true. It is mourning the death of your innocence. It is mourning your dreams. It is loneliness. It is fear. It is anger. The worst part of all is that it becomes your shame. You did not ask for it to happen, but you find your darkness is the shame you carry with you wherever you go. After a while, it becomes a sort of ridiculous armor. You make it a source of strength, because you harden it. You cover it with steel, then you use it to hide. Afterall, you would prefer to no longer be seen as you are in hopes it will keep you from being vulnerable and a victim once again. The darkness of abuse is not the absence of light…it is the ever-present loneliness that in a perverse way becomes our new womb…our protection from the pain that is ultimately going to consume us. We leave our mother's womb and believe life and light are beautiful…only to long for the darkness of the womb once again.

INTRODUCTION

I do not want to overwhelm you with mindless details of my childhood before the abuse; however, it is necessary that you know about my family. I want to make you understand where I came from, because it explains how I dealt with the abuse.

I grew up on a small farm in North Carolina. It had been the birthplace of my dad. I had two older sisters, and was surrounded by my aunts, uncles, and cousins, along with my grandparents. We all worked the farm together…when it was time to plant, we planted; when it was time to reap, we reaped; when it was time to play, we all played. Although there was no reason for anyone to be alone, I often did play alone. I would play and run in the woods. I loved going to the barn just to sit and look down on the garden and simply dream. I loved being alone with my thoughts. More than that, I loved being with my dad. He was so handsome and smart. I was a daddy's girl and didn't care much for primping…to my mother's chagrin. I loved getting dirty and playing with the boys. I would ride motorcycles with them, and anything they attempted, I was going to give it my all to do it as good or better.

My dad made my sisters and me a tree house, which quickly became my home away from home. At approximately the age of seven, he put in an inground pool where he taught me to dive (My dad had taught me to swim at the age of three in a river above a waterfall). I spent a lot of time in the pool swimming; although, it also meant one more chore…keeping it clean was the job of my sisters and me, but it was worth it.

I grew up unafraid to try anything. I learned at my father's side how to ride a motorcycle, a horse, drive a tractor, change the oil in a car, change a tire, and fire a weapon…basically I learned not to be afraid to do things on my own. I was not raised there were jobs for boys and different jobs for girls…no, if you were there, you did whatever needed to be done. I never owned a Barbie in my life… I may have had a baby doll, but my favorite doll was my Mrs. Beasley. She was smart, wore glasses, and was independent. I loved that doll. I did not dream of being a mother or a teacher. I wanted to be a race car driver or ride motocross with the boys.

My mother was beautiful. It's important you know that. She stayed at home with us most of the time; however, she did work at a sewing plant for a while. She loved music. She would sing at church and with her siblings any chance she had. She also played the piano, which she taught me; although, I have lost much of my skills over the years. I was so proud of my mother. She was so talented, and I loved hearing people brag about her.

The most important part of my childhood was our church and our faith. Everything centered around the church I grew up in and the belief that the Bible was the infallible word of God. We never missed a church service. The services were held Sunday morning,

Sunday night, Wednesday night, and Tuesday prayer meeting. We had all-day singings along with food outside near the church meeting place. It seems like a lot, but I never thought of it that way, unless church lasted long into the night, which it did at times. I loved watching Mom sing and play the piano. I loved running around the outside of the church with my cousins and friends…we were happy.

My childhood seemed perfect to me. We were far from rich, but I never went without. I had clothes on my back (Mother made a lot of them), shoes on my feet (when I would wear them), and most importantly…I had love.

Before I get into the heart of my story, can I be real for a moment? I want to be completely honest with you…this is hard for me to write. Because no matter how much therapy you endure, nothing prepares you fully for laying yourself bare…in front of the world…in front of you, my fellow "Sufferers." Is that the right way to describe us? I must be honest; I have struggled with an appropriate word with which to describe us…You and Me. I thought contemporaries might work; however, I didn't feel it was the right word. I thought of "victim," but that wasn't the word either. I simply wanted a word to describe what united us…what made us equal. Well, I believe I have finally discovered the word…it literally just came to mind…we are not "Sufferers" … We are fellow "VICTORS." We are overcomers. We share the same "truth"…a hard "truth." So yes, we have suffered the same torturous secret, but we are more than survivors…we are "VICTORS" … meaning a "conqueror, master, subduer, trimmer, vanquisher, whipper, winner!" We are here having survived and conquered. I realize there may be some of you who are still in the battle, which is the whole purpose of the telling of my story, but I want you to know…you are "VICTORS," even before your battle is over, because I know the strength needed to take the first step…you can overcome this and any other battle you face.

I want you to understand that this is real for me. As I tell you my story, I will feel it. I have learned to walk again, but that doesn't mean what I endured is forgotten. Having said that, I do believe it is important for me to share…why? Because I am living my best life. That is not to say my life is perfect…far from it with the exception that I live in the light. I am no longer ashamed of who I am and what I endured. I am living in a life of freedom, and I want you to know…not from a doctor or a therapist, but from someone who knows the terror and agony… I want you to know that you can survive and dream again. I want you to know that your life was not intended to be lived in darkness covered by the shame in which you had no say in producing. I want you to know you can live a life free of shame and fully in the light, and I want you to know…you deserve it!!

PART ONE

CHAPTER ONE

"Momma, Momma, help me!!!" I screamed as I slept on the sofa. I shared a room with my sister, Pamela, and would often move to the sofa to sleep. It was either late at night or early in the morning that I lay screaming. I was having a nightmare. It was a strange dream. My house was full of people…all women…all who looked exactly like my mother. As I cried screaming begging for my real mother to hold me, I felt her hands on me shaking me, "Wake up, Penny…Wake up!!!" It was my mother rousing me from my sleep. As I came to, I realized it wasn't my mother, but my oldest sister, Darlene. She hugged me and told me everything would be OK. It was then I heard it…Mom was yelling at Dad. Although the door was shut, I could make out what she was saying, although I didn't understand why. As I tried to justify her words, Darlene and I were both shook when we heard something break in their room. I started crying. She told me to stay there, but I followed her and watched her slowly open the door and look in, she closed it quickly, but quietly. She would not tell me what she saw…nor has she ever told me. She took me by the hand and put me in bed with her. I cannot say for sure, but I believe that was the turning point in our relationship. She would be more than my sister…she became my protector.

I must share that this was not the first time I noticed changes in our family. My dad had gotten a job in Charlotte, where he stayed Monday through Friday. It was tough on us kids, but I know it was much harder on my mom. It became clear she was unhappy. As odd as it may sound, the house seemed to take on a darkness along with her sadness. I did not enjoy being in the house. I would stay outside if I possibly could. I remember one afternoon I came home. "Mom!!!" I yelled repeatedly. She never heard me, but I heard her. She was in her bedroom with the door shut. I opened it and saw she was lying on the bed crying uncontrollably. I started to go to her, but felt it was best just to do as Darlene had done and shut the door. Later that evening, my sisters and I were in the kitchen with Mom. I was sitting at the bar while my sister's helped Mom prepare dinner. Daddy would be home shortly. I was so excited I was going to see him…I had almost forgotten about Mom crying. Perhaps it would have been best had I forgotten. Because once I remembered, I asked Mom, "Why were you crying today?"

She looked at me shocked and replied, "I wasn't crying today."

Not catching a clue, I responded, "Yes you were. You were lying on the bed crying."

She replied, "No, I wasn't, Penny!"

Again, not catching a clue, I replied, "Mom, you're lying." Can I just say…I learned a little bit about S.A. (situational awareness); because the next thing that I remember was Mom's hand across my face.

"Don't you ever call me a liar!" Darlene looked at me as if to say, "Do not say another word!" …which I didn't. Pamela just looked shocked. Looking back, I realize Mom was more afraid of my telling Dad that I saw her crying, than she was angry with me. I know this because I saw the shock in my mother's face. It was not anger…it was fear and sadness. I might not have realized it at the time, but I do now.

It was a few months later that I was told my mother was in love with another man. Mom was the one who told me. We had just left the salon. I always went with my mother, because her hairdresser was a relative, and her salon was in her home. I enjoyed playing with her daughter because she was a lot like me. I feel like it is important for me to share these seemingly unimportant details because it allows you to see where my mind was and perhaps give insight into the surprise I felt when we left the salon and Mom, out of the blue, said to me, "Penny," as she took my hand to hold it, "I've fallen in love with another man."

I sat there bewildered as we went down the country road. I was a child, my dad still lived at home with Mom as always, and I'm being told Mom is in love with another man. I must admit, I couldn't look at her because I wasn't sure I understood. She continued, "You know him…you love him. Do you want to know who he is?" I remember feeling numb. I remember thinking about my dad. I might not have understood completely what was happening, but I knew this wasn't right. *Why is she saying this to me?* I thought. Maybe it was because she thought she could trust me, since I never told Dad I saw her crying. Maybe she felt so guilty she needed to confess and hear me say it was OK. But that was not what she received from me. I didn't understand what was happening and I couldn't give her the peace she needed, so without looking at her I said, "No." She was clearly disappointed but said OK, and the topic was not brought up again until an early morning before school.

That morning…I will never forget it! It was on a Monday. My dad would be leaving in a few hours for work. We were never up this early, so I was groggy and irritable…this quickly faded. My sisters and I sat on their bed. Mom and Dad sat across from us.

Mom leaned close and said, "I'm moving out. Your dad will be staying here. We have decided it is best for Darlene to live with your dad, but we are going to give you (meaning Pamela and me) the choice of staying here with your dad or going with me." As I write this, I feel the numbness that took over my body as well as the weight I felt in my head and heart. I wanted to throw up then, and I want to at this moment. It's true that the body never forgets.

Nevertheless, the three of us started crying. I remember holding Pamela's hand. I looked at Daddy. With tears in his eyes, Dad looked at us then moved and sat next to me. As he put his arm around Pamela and me, he looked at Mom and said, "No, this is not fair to them. I won't make them choose. You are the one who wants to leave. They are staying here…in their home."

Mom was clearly distraught. I might not have at the time but looking back I feel so much love and compassion for her, because she was looking at the family, she was about lose…the family she loved. My mother was lost, and she was trapped.

That same morning Mom changed her mind and decided to stay. I remember her telling Daddy she loved him as he walked out the door headed for work, where he would be for the next week. He looked at her. I must be honest; I don't know if he said anything.

Knowing him, he probably told her he loved her too. The truth is my mother did love my dad. I know she did, but she was lost and broken. I also knew my dad was broken.

Things were never the same and eventually my mother quit coming to the house. Which left us, my sisters and me, alone through the week. It also meant Darlene was left as a teenager, to see to it that I got up, got dressed, ate breakfast, and made it to the bus stop. She along with Pamela had to take on the responsibilities of making sure I had dinner and schoolwork was done, as well as baths and bed.

I'm not sure my dad knew we were completely alone...but we were. My sister was.

CHAPTER TWO

The life I had known was gone…forever. I no longer came home to the arms of my mother or my father. I came home to an empty house. I would climb through the window of my bedroom. I kept it unlocked for that purpose; afterall, I was only in third grade and wasn't given a key to the house. It sounds absurd, doesn't it? I wasn't responsible enough to have a key to the house but coming home to an empty house was OK. In fact, it was not OK. It was wrong. I was in third grade and scared. There were times I would go straight to my dad's bed and put the covers over my head until I slept or until the arrival of my sisters from school. I began having vicious nightmares during the day about demons suffocating me. I couldn't breathe. I had been taught in church that the devil had to flee at the mention of the name of Jesus. But during these dreams, I couldn't breathe much less talk…. So, I would say Jesus over and over in my head until I would wake up. You can believe what you will, but I believe I endured these nightmares as a way of teaching me to believe that God was good and where my parents and society had and would fail me, God would protect me. My faith began to be established at that young age. It was established out of necessity…out of loneliness…out of fear. I knew that if God was good, I would be OK.

One thing that remained true and reliable was that my life at home was ever changing. Not only was it not what it had been, it was never the same consistently. It got so that I didn't know who or what I would find when I arrived home daily. I am jumping ahead, but it is almost comical to me. As I am writing this, I am recalling events, which I will share with you; however, I am finding myself laughing out loud at the absurdity of what was about to take place.

As I stated previously, we were left alone; but more than "we," my sister, Darlene, was alone. She was alone with two siblings to care for and no one to help her. I also know that as much as I was aware of what was going on and had happened, Darlene knew much more…she knew things that were traumatic for her. I believe Pamela did as well. You may be asking what happened to my dad… where was he? As I said before, I don't believe he knew we were alone for some time.

Apparently, Mom was supposed to be staying with us most of the time, if not all the time, while Dad was gone through the week. In the beginning she did, but that was short-lived. Regardless, I may have been fighting my demons while sleeping, but Darlene and Pamela were fighting theirs fully awake. Do you understand the concept of needing family…i.e., needing to belong? Every story about gang members begins with this concept…this idea…this truth. But this reality does not apply only to inner city kids; it applies to all kids…even a farm girl, who is left to care for her two younger siblings. My sister needed help. She needed to belong. She needed to escape.

It may be at this point that you are asking yourself about my sister, Pamela. Well, the truth is, Pamela was quiet. She was living her own personal hell that I was not aware of until later. In fact, she doesn't remember a lot of things, because I believe she was completely lost, and was spared the agony of her memories. As hard as it is for me to think about what Darlene was going through, the quietness of Pamela, brings me to my knees because as an adult, I realize she was suffering a pain that was unspeakable. Her loneliness, no doubt surmounted mine, and it sincerely breaks my heart when I think about it now. Just to make you aware, I will not share all of Pamela's story nor will I share all of Darlene's, because they are simply not mine to share. I will only tell what I believe is relevant to my story…just know, they were always there…always present for me.

Let me move on…. As I stated previously, things were changing almost daily. Mom moved into a tiny two-room trailer with Roger. Roger was the man with whom my mother fell in love. She was right…I did know him…I knew him well. His son was my best friend, and our families were close. Mom sang in a group with him at our church as well as other churches. He was ten years younger than her. I'm not sure why my mother was attracted to him, other than their love of music; however, he was the one she left my dad for, and he left his wife for my mother. I didn't see his son again until I was an adult.

I saw my mother less and less; however, I noticed she was extremely skinny. My mother told me as an adult about the time my dad showed up at their trailer. She told me he walked in…looked at her and Roger, went to the tiny kitchen, opened the refrigerator, walked over to Roger, took out one thousand dollars and said, "Go buy my wife some food." There is so much I would like to interject about this scene, but I don't feel it would be coming from a place where I want to live in my heart and mind, and I won't go there, except to say it profoundly affected my mom. According to her, she realized what she had lost and sadly she lived with it for the rest of her life through the Grace God had shown her.

Along with seeing Mom rarely, other changes were taking place. Darlene found her "family." It came two-fold…first, through drugs and alcohol, secondly through drug addicts. I must be very sensitive here. I want you to understand what is absurd about this very idea that they were my sister's "family" is that they also became my family. Two of the men, became as brothers to me. If my sister wasn't home, they would make me something to eat and sometimes help me with my homework. I would talk to them about my day at school and they would listen. If someone was mean, they would cuss and ask if I wanted them to hit the person. It's so funny to remember, because they were talking about punching a third grader. I remember swimming in the pool as they sat on the patio making sure I was OK, drinking a beer and smoking cigarettes. What kind I don't know, but they were going to make sure I didn't drown. If I were posting this on Facebook, I would interject a LOL right here; because truthfully, I would have saved them from drowning before they saved me. Having said that, if anything had happened to me in their care, Darlene would have killed them, and they knew it. I felt safe…neither of them nor any of Darlene's friends made me feel anything but cared for and truthfully, it was far better than coming home to an empty house.

This was my life. It worked to fill part of the void, but it didn't change the fact that no one could come home with me and I mostly played alone, usually in the woods. I even cleaned spaces and created a makeshift house using sticks and wood as furniture. I still sat at the barn and dreamt. I would ride motorcycles (if Daddy was home) but as life progressed in this manner, I found that it was becoming too unbearable for me take, so I started a separate life in my head. What I mean by this is I started lying to people at school about my life at home, and when possible, I would make as much of my life as normal as I could possibly do on my own. On the weekends, I would walk to my grandparents and watch TV with them until it was bedtime. I would call Dad to let him know I was walking home. Sometimes, he would meet me. I loved walking at night alone even at that age. I know it's hard to understand, but it felt normal, and nothing about my life was normal. I craved glimpses of it. Working in the garden, mowing the grass, and anything having to do with the farm or hanging out in the woods became the best part of my life.

The hardest thing I had ever faced, up to this point, was realizing there was no normal left for me…at least as I knew it and believed it to be. I discovered this the day I walked into my grandmother's back door and heard her and my aunts talking about my sisters and me. They were concerned about how we would turn out if things didn't change. I thought to myself, *I'm still Penny!!!! I've done nothing wrong!!* They never knew I had walked in and heard them. I knew I was innocent, but more than anything I knew God was good and because he was good…I would be as well.

This paragraph may seem random, but it is necessary for you to know. My dad started coming home often. Darlene was in and out but seemed to be changing as well. Her friends changed. This change happened suddenly and out of the blue as far as I was concerned. I had later found out that Daddy had been told what was going on while he was away. Dad did not know we were alone. It was a lot for him to travel back and forth every day, but in the end, it was part of what saved us. I later heard that my sister was at a house for drug users. My dad found out and went to get his daughter. Although he was threatened with violence should he enter, he went in…my dad had to look for her because she was hiding; however, he did bring her home… Darlene had finally been heard. Someone finally noticed her torment, and it was her dad.

It wouldn't be long before Darlene would give her heart to Christ and marry her childhood friend, Don. He would later join the Navy and they would move to Florida…among other places. My sister never did drugs again and never looked back, other than to take care of me…which she still does to this very day. At the age of fifty-two years old, my sister still worries about me, cares for me and would do anything to make sure I'm safe, happy, and never alone. She is a complete miracle. As you will soon realize, we all are. There are so many roads I could have gone down that would have destroyed my life, but God continued to make sure I kept my faith in him.

CHAPTER THREE

I'll never forget the day I met the woman that would change my life. I was playing in the woods by the house when Dad pulled in driving a little white convertible. The passenger seat held a woman with long black hair. She was thin, stylishly dressed, with huge gold rings with stones. I thought she was beautiful. I assumed the car Daddy was driving was hers, and I was correct. Dad seemed a bit nervous and excited to introduce me. She was formal in a way I wasn't used to. I can't imagine what she must have thought about me…I would discover that later.

Her name was Ella, and she was the woman my dad would eventually marry. Ella was a widow whose husband had been killed overseas. She had five children: however, only four lived with her. The oldest son was married. The other four lived with Ella. The oldest was a boy who was older than Pamela, but younger than Darlene. Two of the girls were slightly older than me but younger than Pamela and Darlene and the younger daughter was a year or so younger than me.

I was excited about having more siblings. I thought it would be like the Brady Brunch. There were glimpses in the beginning that could have been equated to the Brady Bunch, but they were extremely rare and far between. The hardest part for me was moving from my home to Ella's house. I found out on a Sunday afternoon at my grandparents. Daddy was telling everyone we would be moving. I yelled, "I'm not going!"

Daddy said, "It's just a house. It's not our home."

I walked to the door, I turned and yelled, "It's my home!" I don't know if I had ever raised my voice to my dad, but I felt myself sink. It was a terrible feeling. I left and went to the barn then walked in the woods. It was inevitable that we would move into their house, and eventually move back into the house that I had called home, but it would never be my home again.

I won't go into much detail about my life with Ella and her kids. I will only say this…my stepmother was nothing of a mother to me. She was not kind. She was not loving. She was hard and would ensure that we would never be able to call her house our home.

Years went by, and we endured. What I learned growing up in the way I did is that God always provided what was needed at any given time. He's never late, even though there were times I questioned him about his timeline. One of the best things he did for me was bring a friend into my life that would be there through everything; although, you wouldn't have known that by the way we met.

Daddy and Ella separated, and we moved back to the house I grew up in and started back to the original school I had attended, where my sister and her husband stayed with Pamela and I while Daddy was at work. Although I had grown up there, I was still considered the "new girl" in school. I was in sixth grade and my best friend was Zenja Brown. Some of the seventh and eighth-grade girls didn't like me because the cutest boy in school had noticed me. I received word at lunch that I was supposed to go to the bathroom where they would, I guessed, "beat me up." So, during lunch, I got up and went to the girl's bathroom, with Zenja by my side. It was packed with girls. There were two ring leaders who were beginning to yell at me, when the principal came in and broke it up, but before she did, I remember vividly looking up and seeing this beautiful, blonde girl looking over the door of a stall. She apparently was standing on a toilet. It may not have seemed possible, but I knew she and I would become friends. It wasn't until the following year on the school playground that she approached me and apologized. She said that she had been the new girl prior to my arriving, and she was just thankful the attention was off her. I must laugh here. I didn't blame her.

By this time, Ella and her kids had moved back in with us at the house where I was raised. Things were worse than ever. But it was Heidi who stayed by my side and supported me. She was witness to my life at home. She didn't have to call me her best friend, but she did, and she was mine. To this very day, I know she is still my best friend. You see, not many people would have wanted to be a part of my life. But Heidi wasn't just anyone, she was special with a capacity to love and show compassion (Heidi will read this and disagree and say it was all me, but it was her). Heidi was very popular and came from a very affluent family, although you would never know it. They were so down to earth. She and her family loved me. Gail, Heidi's mom, treated me like I belonged. She would make me help clean up the house or dishes. I loved it! It felt normal. They took me on trips with them. I ate in my first fine-dining restaurant with her family, where I learned what escargot was, and I learned to snow-ski on another trip.

Heidi's friendship and her loyalty to me, given my circumstances, were unshakable. That kind of friendship is rare. Amongst other people who were in my life, my uncle Bill, was so valuable to me. Anytime he made homemade sweet tea, he would invite me to have some. It seems so simple, but it meant he noticed me and cared. He still shows that kind of love to me to this very day. He and my aunt Patsy would have me for dinner often. My cousin, Joanne, and I would hang out…tan too often, but these were some of the people I must mention, as it is important for you know that God didn't fail me. He always provided what I needed to get me through. There are others that God put into my life that you will learn about and know their importance in ensuring my life didn't completely derail. However, I wanted to mention these few as I am going to fast-forward.

It was the night of Pamela's high school graduation. Pamela had come home from school to find she had been locked out of the house. Let me say this is hard to write, as it is, hard to remember the pain she went through, but it is necessary for you to know about this day. She left and went to Martha and Nathan's house. Martha and Nathan had been dear friends of my parents when I was growing up. We were not related to them, but they are every bit our family. I had known them as far back as I can remember. Nathan always made me want to be better than I was. Martha made me want to be a good mother and keep a clean house; however, the last statement didn't quite take. I must laugh writing that because Nathan used to tell the story how he hated to see me coming, because he knew I would make a mess or break something. He told the story how as a small child, I was on the tractor messing with it. He said I took a piece off that had he and my dad tried with tools would not have been able to accomplish what I had done. I loved Nathan. He is no longer on this earth, but I'm sure I'll get to heaven, and he will have told those stories prior to my arrival. Later, I discovered from my teachers that he had gone to my open houses and parent teacher conferences when no one else would have been there. A blessing doesn't begin to share what he and Martha meant to me and my sisters. I attribute anything good about me in part to these two.

As I was saying, Pamela had come home to a locked house…yes, they were there and wouldn't let her in. She went to Martha and Nathan's and stayed. Later that day, we were able to get in and took two small garbage bags and put our things in them. You would think based on the amount of clothing and shoes in the house that we would have more. No, none of them were ours. Nevertheless, that evening we sat with Daddy. Pamela was on one side of him, and I was on the other side. Pamela had tears in her eyes, leaning on Dad's chest. I told him we were moving in with Martha and Nathan. I said, "We can't take it anymore!"

Ella walked in and said, "What can't you take anymore, Penny?" I walked over to her. I told her we could no longer take living the way we were living. She asked, "What do you want?"

I responded, "We only wanted you to love us." I guess I was yelling because Daddy called me down. Pamela and I left after this and moved into Martha and Nathan's home for several weeks. Perhaps it was even longer. Eventually, we went to live with my grandparents.

This would prove to be one of the best things to happen to me to encourage the faith I already had in my loving Father. We read the Bible every night, watched wholesome TV and never missed Billy Graham. I helped my Paw Paw in the garden and Maw Maw in the kitchen. Daddy was there every weekend visiting us. He gave Maw

Maw money to buy what we needed. He had no idea what life had been like for us. Maw Maw said he cried when she showed him what we had brought with us. Nevertheless, our move had been the best for us. The only problem was I started putting on weight because my grandmother would make these enormous meals, which I had to eat…what a problem to have…right? However, had I not, she would have worried that something was wrong with me. Pamela stayed for a while, then moved into her own place and eventually in with Don and Darlene in Florida. I was always able to call them anytime I needed them…which I did need them.

PART TWO

CHAPTER FOUR

Iwalked out of the restroom. I went to the water fountain to take a sip of water before returning. As I turned from the water fountain, he grabbed me, pushed me against the wall. He was trying to kiss me as I felt him touching me. It felt as though I was dangling there unable to touch the floor. I felt his hand touching my breast. I felt his body pushing against mine. I struggled as he tried to kiss me. I mustered all the strength I had and punched him in his left side with my right fist. He let me go. As I ran to the swinging doors, I heard him saying… "I'll give you a piece of gum." I stumbled through the doors that would lead me back into the sanctuary of the Church I attended. I was an early twelve years old. I sat in the back of the church shaking, wondering what had just happened. What was that? I knew this man. He not only attended my church, but he worked at my school. I would joke with him and laugh. He always gave me a piece of gum. I sat there wondering and asking repeatedly…*What just happened?*

As I left, all I wanted to do was tell someone, but something told me not to…I would be blamed in some way…it would be my fault! So…I kept it to myself; however, I did eventually tell Darlene. It was the first time something like this would happen, but it would not be the last.

A couple of months went by, and I was attending another church of a similar faith. I walked into church and was standing off to the side alone. An older man walked up to me (a man who knew me), put his arm around me and stuck his hand down my shirt and grabbed my breast. You may be asking, why didn't I scream or yell? Well, I knew it wouldn't matter. I was a child, and I would inevitably be blamed. I couldn't do that to my grandparents either. My grandmother worried about me enough, without me adding to it. I was blessed to be in her home. Besides, it wasn't anything I couldn't handle. Aside from a little humiliation, I would be OK. I simply had to look past these events and the others that would occur…at least that's what I told myself, but the fact that I noticed men looking at me in a way that often made me uncomfortable could not always be ignored. As much as I wanted to be a normal pre-teen, like Heidi and Joanne, there was no escaping the fact that I never would be. I started seeing the world differently. Where they felt comfortable in their skin, I felt nothing of the sort. I matured early…physically. I hated it!!

To say I hated it is an understatement. From that point on I would wear bras that fit too tight so they would hold me as to prevent anyone from noticing my breasts. I would literally have my breasts almost tucked underneath my armpits so to not bring attention to me. I tried to hide my body behind clothes too big for me. I didn't want anyone to see my shape. I'm fifty-two years old and I still find that I'm more comfortable that way. I'm slowly coming out of the "hiding my body" mentality, but it is a journey.

I'm still amazed at how the things of our childhood fix on future selves. But they truly do. Through my "Learning to Walk Again" journey, I had to nurture my inner child. I still must talk to her about clothes I wear. I also must remind her of her strength…I must remind her she is not a victim and shame does not belong with her. I had to and still do remind her she is not alone, but it makes sense this is an ongoing battle, because I often felt alone. Even if I was surrounded by people, I felt as though I lived alone with my thoughts and prayers. My nightmares were an unending presence. They were all the same… the demons would try and suffocate me. I would try to scream. I would try to move. But it was only when I said the name of Jesus that I would wake up. They became so violent that I was often afraid to go to sleep.

I started putting a Bible underneath my pillow. I would pretend to hug and kiss him good night. I would ask him to protect me once again. There were times I would begin to feel the presence of the dream before I would even go to sleep. I wasn't sure what else I could do to combat what I was going through. In the meantime, I would read my Bible and pray often. I went to church every time the doors were open. I would always listen intently to the preacher. I wanted so much for someone to tell me what to do without having to share what was going on with anyone.

One service I heard the preacher speak about Solomon. God told him to ask for anything and he would have it. So, Solomon asked for Wisdom to lead his people. God told him, because he had asked for the good thing, he would bless Solomon with wisdom, family, and wealth beyond measure, and God did that very thing he had promised. I have asked for wisdom and discernment every day since hearing that message. I had been taught that God was the same today, yesterday, and forever. I believed if it was what pleased God, then it would please him at that time and now.

As I continued my life and continued to fight my demons, I spent a lot of time with Heidi, but I was also spending more time with my mom. I stayed with her and Roger regularly. I would also attend their church occasionally. My grandmother was never happy about my going to her house and staying the night. I would have to check in with her often. I don't know why she felt so insecure about my going to mom's, but she did. She eventually told me it was OK if I didn't see her. She said God would understand if I didn't fully honor my mother. I know she meant well. She was speaking out of love and concern for me. I told her everything was OK. I would try not to stay more than a night or two, because it worried her so much.

As far as the rest of my life, Dad came to see me every weekend. He almost always had Ella with him. I didn't really care. I was always happy to see him. My dad loved me. I simply had to accept that things had changed for us…this was our relationship.

I also spent time helping my grandfather in the garden. I helped my grandmother with dinner and clean up. My nights with my grandparents were the best. We would watch *Jeopardy* and *Wheel of Fortune* every night. We also watched a lot of Westerns. At night, my grandmother and I would make a snack of fresh tomatoes, cucumbers, and onions from the garden, along with cheese. Maw Maw and Paw Paw were saints. I learned how love and how commitment worked through watching them. They would pester each other in a loving way. My

Paw Paw would grab my grandmother and tell her to dance a jig with him in the kitchen. They competed with one another, especially when watching game shows. But the most profound thing they did was simply hold hands while they sat in their recliners; then they would get on their arthritic knees and pray for one another and their family every night, and when I walked by their room at night, it would look as if there was only one person in their king-size bed. They did everything within their power to ensure I had a reasonably normal life but teaching me what a lifelong love looked like was the most beautiful gift they gave me. I will forever be grateful for the love shown me every day I lived with them.

CHAPTER FIVE

I sat there wondering how I could allow myself to get into this position. My heart was pounding. I had accepted a ride from someone I knew, although barely. He was the twenty-three-year-old son of a preacher who was at the campground. He wasn't alone. He had a friend with him, so I got in the back seat. I shouldn't have taken the ride when it was offered, but it was hot, and I didn't want to walk any farther. Now, I sat there on the bed where they told me to sit and wait. They had told me they had to make a quick stop before taking me back to the camp. I knew something was wrong. I knew from the moment I got into the car. I had asked them to drop me off that I had changed my mind, but they told me not to worry…it wouldn't take long.

I noticed my hands moving. I would hold them together, then cup them. I wanted to run, but I seemed to be frozen…afraid to breathe, afraid to speak. I had felt this feeling before, but not to this extreme. I could hear them talking. I wasn't sure what they were saying to one another. I knew music was playing from the portable radio/cassette player…or "boom box." It was as though my mind wouldn't shut down long enough for me to understand either of them or the music. I sat on the bed, and they sat in the two chairs by the window, which was covered by a dark, thick, flower covered curtain, smoking pot. *Why can't I move?* I asked myself. Everything inside me screamed, "RUN" but I couldn't. I felt my chest pound. I almost hoped it would explode.

He walked over to me…the one I knew. He sat beside me. He put his hand on my leg and told me to relax. He offered me some pot…I said no. I felt his hand move up my inner thigh underneath my dress. He told me to lay down. I said I was fine, but he insisted. He slowly and steadily pushed me to my back. His friend kept looking at me. I tried desperately to keep from looking at either of them. He told me not to worry about anything, just do what he said. I felt my underwear being removed. I couldn't speak. He kissed me. I felt pain and pressure like I'd never known. He pushed and pushed…pressure and pressure! I wanted it to stop.

Please stop!! I cried in my head. I just wanted it over. I turned my head toward the music. I tried to focus on the music…. Van Halen was playing. I could feel my insides ripping apart. I wanted it to end!!! Finally, it was over. He got up and to my horror I realized it wasn't over. His friend said it was his turn. I had not been able to speak up to this point, but I managed to say in a whisper, "Please…no." The last thing I remember was looking at the two chairs and feeling a tear flow down my face.

I woke up in a dormitory in the camp where I was staying. I was covered in blood to my knees. I showered off quickly, worried someone would realize I had been gone. Of course, they did, and I was fussed at for being gone. Everyone had been looking for me. I could see they were deeply concerned. I apologized and told them I had fallen asleep in the old dormitory. Why didn't I tell them? Because I would prefer that they think that than for them to get mad at me for getting into the car with two men. Afterall, who would believe me? This man was well known, and his father was one of the leaders of our church. I was a nobody…a kid. Also, what would my grandparents think? I simply had to forget it…keep it bottled up.

This would prove to be impossible as I had clearly been injured in some way. I had started bleeding that day and after six months, I was still bleeding. I was beginning to get sick. I guess I was anemic. I started sleeping on the living room sofa. I can't exactly say why, but I know I was scared. My grandmother had become quite worried about me. She or I one called Darlene and told her what was going on, and either she or my grandmother told my dad. I clearly had to be seen by a doctor. An appointment was made, and Dad and Ella took me to the doctor, a gynecologist. I had never been to one and this proved to be quite traumatic for me. I was in the office alone with a nurse and the doctor, when the doctor did his examination.

Afterwards, he asked me something that at that time I couldn't understand. He asked if I was having sex. I emphatically said, "NO!" At that time, I was not aware of the hymen, which had clearly indicated to him through the examination that I had had sex. He never asked any other questions. I can only assume he thought I was lying. Once again, I fell through the cracks and was unjustly judged. It makes me so angry when I think about it now. I was twelve years old, and he simply assumed I was lying. It didn't occur to him to ask serious questions. He failed me!!

I was put on birth control to help regulate the bleeding. But let's add insult to injury…I went to school the following week. I was in eighth grade. I was on the playground, when my friend, Tammy, came up to me and said, "Penny, your stepsisters are going around telling everyone you had to be put on birth control because you're having sex." I wanted to cry but I simply told Tammy it was just a lie. You see, even though I didn't live with them, I still attended the same school. Regardless of their motive in putting me down, there was only one way they could have known about this…through Ella. I knew they enjoyed getting to me, so I developed an attitude of "you can't hurt me and if you do, you will be the last person to ever know it." I would never allow them to see my suffering because it would bring them too much joy.

As they say, time heals all wounds…right? Well, as far as I was concerned, I believed it did. What I didn't realize was…time "bottles up" all wounds. I had simply learned to live with what life had given me. I had to believe there was something better in store for me because God would not have put me here for this to be my life. He loved me. I didn't doubt that for one second. My faith was firmly in him and his word. Again, if God was good, then He would take care of me and bring me to something I would be eventually proud of calling my life.

Life seemed to normalize. I got my first job at the age of fourteen as a waitress at the local convenience store slash "greasy spoon." I had a normal boyfriend at fifteen and eventually he broke my heart and is to this day married to the girl for which he broke up with me. Although he was a good guy, he is one of those that I thank God for my unanswered prayer.

I dated other guys and moved to a different job when I was sixteen. I worked as a cashier at the local Winn Dixie. It was just down the hill from the high school, so it was easy for me to go from school straight to work. The pain of my past was just that…the past.

CHAPTER SIX

The phone was ringing. I rushed from my room to the living room to answer it, as my grandparents were out of the house. I said, "Hello." The man on the other end attended my church. I said, "I'm sorry but Maw Maw and Paw Paw are not here, can I take a message?" He responded, "I didn't call to speak with your grandparents. I called to ask if you would be interested in making some money?"

I said, "Of course…what do you need me to do?" What came next was shocking.

He asked, "I'm here at the house alone and wondered if you would be willing to come over and give me a body massage?" I semi-laughed and said, "I don't think so."

He said, "I'm serious, Penny. I'm already naked and will pay you well." He said it exactly like that…it was a "matter of fact" statement. I hung up. I was shaking. I may have thrown up. I can't say for sure, but my body at this moment is feeling extremely nauseous.

Do you remember that I told you I had successfully bottled up my past? Well, it must have been a champagne bottle, because that was the last shake of the champagne bottle, and the cork blew. I could no longer take the pain of this life. I don't remember getting it out of the drawer, but I remember putting the tip of the knife to my chest. I wanted my heart to stop hurting. I didn't want to feel this pain any longer. The knife was quite sturdy with a thick long blade. I felt the resistance of my sternum. I put both hands on the end of the knife, but realized it was too unsteady. I tried bending down on the counter, thinking I would fall on it…this would surely push it through.

Realizing none of these ideas would push it through my chest, I decided to push it between my ribs. I put the knife between two ribs. My plan was to push up and toward my heart. As I started to do this, I had what seemed like a vision of my grandparents finding me there dead from her knife. I envisioned my dad, mom, and my sisters finding out. I could feel their grief and I didn't think they would ever fully recover. I put the knife down and became angry. I wasn't just angry, I was enraged. *This is not fair!!!* I thought. Then it hit me…GOD!! I was angry, but not at just anyone…I was angry with God. I had believed he was good. I had trusted him to take care of me. I had given him my life only to have him fail me once again. I thought, God wasn't good! Had he been good, then he would have given me a break. I was simply on this earth to be used and hurt. Well, since God wasn't going to do anything about it, then I would. First on my list was to get God out of my life!

The faith that I was brought up in said that drinking and smoking was a sin, because it hurt the body. Since I was only sixteen years old, I could not buy alcohol, but I could buy cigarettes, and that's exactly what I did. I went behind my grandparent's house and lit the first cigarette. I stood there looking at the chickens and the rooster that woke me up every morning. Then I took the fingers that held the cigarette between them and pointed up to heaven and said,

"God, I'm through with you, and to prove it, I am going to smoke this entire pack of cigarettes!!" It's OK if you laugh at this, just remember I believed I was sinning, and this would get God out of my life. I was serious. The problem was I didn't want to smoke the one cigarette, much less the entire pack of cigarettes. The other problem was I couldn't just not believe. When I was in therapy years later, the therapist asked me, "What would happen if you were not good?"

I told him, "God had to be good and if he was good, I had to be good. If I choose a life contrary to my belief, then I would be broken."

He asked, "What's wrong with being broken?"

I said, "If I was broken, then I would no longer be on this planet...I would have taken my life."

What was I to do? My friend, Donna, had invited me to church that night. It was a church I did not attend; however, they were having a guest speaker from Georgia. I put the cigarette out and looked to heaven and said, "God, I am going to church tonight. If you are there and you really love me, then show me tonight. If you do, I will serve you for the rest of my life."

That night Donna picked me up and we drove to a town approximately forty-five minutes away. When we arrived, I sat in the second row to the back right corner. I wanted to cry from the minute I walked in, and I felt love, but I would not allow that to be enough. I don't remember what the preacher said during his sermon. I was so nervous. I was afraid I would leave with no clarity. That scared me more than anything. The sermon was over, and he had turned the podium over to the actual pastor of the church. The pastor was about to pray the final prayer, when the visiting speaker stood up and walked over to the pastor and said something to him. The visiting speaker walked to the podium and looked in my direction.

He said, "I need you to come to the front…God has something he wants to say to you." The church was wall-to-wall people, so although I thought he was talking to me, I didn't move. I looked around me waiting for someone to stand up and move to the front, but he pointed at me and said, "You, young lady, in the back corner." I stood up and went to the front. He reiterated, "God has something he wants to say to you. He wants you to know he heard you today. He wants you to know that he has always been with you and will never let you go. He knows the pain you have endured and will see you through the pain you still will endure. He said to tell you he has a purpose for your life if you have faith in him. He will never leave you and will direct your life."

I fell…literally! I was overcome with emotion and gratitude. My life changed that day. I must tell you I have not always made the right choices. I have added grief to my life; however, I can say with one-hundred percent certainty that God has never failed me. He has never disappointed me. He has in fact brought me through more pain and suffering, but God never promised me my life would be without pain and suffering. I can honestly say I wouldn't change how my life evolved, as it has molded me into the person, I am today… Beautifully imperfect, totally flawed but wonderfully cared for and loved beyond measure!

Years later I was in a group therapy session. Having heard my story up to this point, a woman in the group asked, "How is it that you still have faith in God? Why didn't you give up your faith in him? It would only make sense."

I responded, "I didn't give up faith in God, but I did give up faith in Christians." I continue to have faith in a Christian, meaning individuals; however, simply because someone calls themselves "Christian" does not in any way give them my confidence. I have seen so much hate from self-described "Christians," when the truth is simply that my Savior never displayed hate in any form. I realize this will offend some, but my faith should never be in an individual simply because they profess Christ. Understand that when I think of Christ, I think of someone who showed love…true love to all people regardless of who they were.

Galatians 3:28 says, "There is no Greek nor Jew, no male nor female, no slave nor free…." Philippians 2:1–11 states, "who though he was in the form of God did not count equality with God as something to be exploited, but emptied himself in the form of a servant, even to the point of death on a cross." He also showed men how to treat women and children, who were seen as less than that of men in those days. My faith is exactly where it should…in God!

Life continued as life does, but I had a new foundation with which to face it. I was trusting God, but the fact was, I still had not dealt with the abuse. I simply put the cork back in the champagne bottle that was my life; however, my faith was a nice cool place to store it. It would be fine, and should it show its ugly face, I would remember God had it and I was OK. There is a lot of truth in this…I do believe God can fully heal someone; however, the kind of hurt I was dealing with had infiltrated my body, my mind (although masked) … and my spirit. Time would prove that I would have to face the demons of my past…but not yet. I would have more that I would have to deal with before that happened. Let's just say the bottle was secure in the cool place where which I kept it, but bubbles were forming and inevitably the cork would give and there would be a mess that could no longer be put back into the bottle. I would have to face it. It would become something I would no longer be able to keep safe. My faith would be tested once again, but once again God would prove faithful.

CHAPTER SEVEN

Where shall I begin? I had recorked my demons in the champagne bottle that was my life; however, I need you to be fully aware of the fact that I was living my life in shame. I had told you about the shame that becomes the hiding place for those who are victims of sexual abuse. I pretended I was living in the light, but I was nowhere near it. You see, I had the secrets of darkness that I continued to carry with me everywhere. The longing I had to be normal or at least appear normal consumed my life. I would often pretend my life was better than it was. No one in school knew what my life was truly like, and I learned to carry myself in such a way to show people I was confident. Confident like Heidi, and my other friends. Yet inside, I was living in the darkness of the womb I had created for myself. Yes, my faith was in God, but I had not dealt with my demons…the evil of my past.

On the outside, I appeared to be a healthy, happy teenager. I worked a lot and went to school. I dated and hung out with friends, but I often felt alone and completely inadequate. To make matters worse, my grandparents were struggling with my long workdays. I came home late from the restaurant I was working at to find my grandmother quite upset. She said it was too much for them to worry about me being out late. Yes, I had called and told her I had to work late, but I had the feeling she didn't believe me. I explained the inspector came and would not even rate the restaurant. He said he would be returning the next morning. If things were not brought up to code, the restaurant would be shut down; therefore, I had to stay and clean. Although it was true, I realized it truly was too much for my grandparents having me there. What was I going to do? I had nowhere to go. There was no way I would move in with Daddy if he was married to Ella. That left me with one option…my mom.

This is difficult to share as it was difficult to do…I had to ask my mother if I could live with her and Roger. I remember the moment I asked her. She looked at me for a moment and I began to cry. For that moment, I felt total rejection and fear. But she put her arms around me and said yes, but she would have to talk to Roger. I did eventually move in with them. The move went well, until my then boyfriend and Roger had a major argument over a business matter. Roger did not like him, and my boyfriend didn't like Roger. Mom tried to convince me to break up with him, but I would not. This proved to add a lot of stress to our relationship. Later, another disagreement occurred between Mom, Roger, and me. I didn't realize how bad it was until the day my friend drove me home to find all my belongings were in my car. She looked at me confused and said, "Penny, what's going on?"

I responded with, "I guess I am no longer welcome here."

She asked, "What are you going to do?" I responded that I would be fine. I told her goodbye, but the truth was, I didn't know what I was going to do. I had nowhere to go. I sat in my car surrounded by clothes, stuffed animals I had on my bed, a few photos, and school memorabilia. I drove to the convenience store and used the payphone outside and called my sister, Darlene. She said she would take care of it. The next day my sister told me my aunt Doris would love for me to move in with her.

My aunt Doris is a complete saint. I don't know what I would have done without her. She made sure I felt completely at home. She showed me an unbelievable amount of love. She loved my boyfriend, Jeff. She spoiled him whenever he would come over. I remember once, we were all watching TV. She told me I needed to get up and get Jeff something to drink. I responded by telling her he knew where the refrigerator was…of course, I was not being disrespectful because we all started laughing. However, I still didn't get him a drink…he was happy to get it himself. I'm sharing this with you because she did all she could do to give me a home…some normalcy.

So, here I was in a new place that once again God had provided for me. I learned so much from every situation I found myself in. I learned how to care, I learned how to give to those who need a helping hand. I learned God never fails, but I learned that above all things… love matters most. Things are simply things, and love is simply a word whose meaning is given only by another person. I'm so truly grateful for the love that I was shown throughout my dysfunctional life. The love shown to me has made me the person I am. I have said it before, and I mean it from the depths of my very soul…I would do it all again to end up the person I am today. I know the joy of life lived in the service of others, because I needed the service of others.

I know and understand the importance of love. I know what faith and faithfulness mean and I know the importance of both. I will forever be grateful for the gift of the life, knowledge, and wisdom God has given through his protective hand in my life. However, having said that, it took years to get me where I am today. It took asking for help. The kind of suffering that I went through and possibly what you are going through is like a nightmare…a cold, dark, gloomy, lonely nightmare. I simply want you to know that you can live life full of light and joy. It takes work, but first it takes asking for help. Up to this point in my story, I had not asked for help. That would come and it would prove to be the best thing to happen to me.

CHAPTER EIGHT

I am going to skim over my life to get us to the point I want to share with you. I graduated from high school. I started nursing school almost immediately after graduation. I was working third shift in a cotton mill. When I left the mill, I would go straight to McDonald's and get the tills ready for the day, then I would shower and go to school. I was set up for failure. I eventually broke up with Jeff and moved to Charleston to live with my sister while I attended school. I worked part time at the fitness center on the Air Force base as well as a waitress at the Non-Commissioned Officer's Club, and occasionally the Officer's Club. It was perfect for me because I could study and work. I had no plans to get married or have children. I dated, but usually one and done. I did date a guy for a few months. He lived on the Battery in Charleston. If you're familiar with the area you know it is an affluent "old money" area of Charleston. The guy I was dating was a likable guy who played professional tennis. I really was not thinking of us past our next date; however, it hurt when he told me he could never be serious with me because I didn't come from the right family. Of course, I didn't see him again even after he kept calling asking to speak with me. I didn't care…he was out.

I continued to have varying interactions with men, some were positive, but some were heartbreaking. There was a man whom I had met where I worked, who asked me to move to Maine to be near him. He wanted to put me up in an apartment and pay for my education as well as give me an annual salary…if I was there for him when he wanted me. I don't believe I have to go into detail about what he meant.

I suppose I don't have to tell you why I gave up on the idea of being loved or loving anyone…that is until the day John walked in the door of the gym where I worked. He was tall and very handsome. He smiled at me but didn't say a word. I went to the phone, called Heidi, who was back in North Carolina, and told her I had just seen the man I was going to marry. I didn't see him again for a month, but I knew I would marry him. Then one day I turned a corner and saw him working out with his friend. We both smiled and said hello. Then as he was leaving, he stopped, introduced himself and asked if I would like to join him and his friends at the Charleston Downs that following Saturday…John and I were married six months later.

He was diagnosed with stage four melanoma. If you are familiar with it, then you know his prognosis was not good. We moved to Texas so he would have access to the care he needed. We made the most of the days we had together. We had a baby girl, Mary Elizabeth, a year later. He passed away shortly after her first birthday. I recently gave Mary a letter I wrote her while she was in the crib sleeping. I was telling her she would be OK, but John would be leaving us to go to be with Jesus. As I read it again, I broke down and cried because I had so many emotions pinging off every part of my body. I was scared. I was responsible for this baby, and I was only twenty-two years old. What I haven't told you is I had lied to John about my age, knowing this then twenty-seven-year-old officer would never have taken me out had I been honest with him and told him I had just turned twenty. The day he told me he loved me, I told him my age. It wasn't lost on me how wrong it was for me to have lied to him. I remember he was so angry with me. I told him I understood if he wanted to end our relationship. His response was, "Well, it's too late now…I'm in love with you." I'm finding myself smiling because once he got over being angry with me, we laughed about it and spent a wonderful evening together.

After John passed away, I moved from Texas back to Charleston to be close to my sisters so they could help me while I went back to school. My friends encouraged me to start dating, which I did; however, I didn't expect to fall in love again. I was so protective of Mary and therefore she was my priority. I did, however, meet someone I fell in love with and knew I could trust…I met Charles. John's friends had introduced me to him. Charles and I were married, and several years later, we had another beautiful daughter, Taylor Kathleen. Charles adopted Mary Elizabeth when he realized he had no real rights to her if I should die. He loved her, and so he gave her something not every man would have done…he gave her a father…a dad.

We spent a wonderful twenty-two years together happily married while traveling the world with his military career as the catalyst. After he retired, we moved to Nashville to be close to his family. Sadly, the marriage ended in divorce; however, there will always be a great deal of love and respect shared for one another. I will forever be grateful for our life together as a married couple, our life we share with our kids, and one day, our grandchildren. One thing for certain about life and living…it is always changing.

So…there I was…divorced, empty nester, and alone. What a mix! I was devasted. My confidence was shot. I was making terrible choices. I was drinking entirely too much, and I started dating but quickly realized I didn't know what I was doing. I had no business dating when I had so much that needed to be addressed in my life. I did start seeing a therapist after visiting my doctor and telling him, "I need help!"

Anyway, I saw my therapist several days a week. She helped me through the divorce. After almost a year, I opened up about my rape and abuse. She was surprised at first. She commented on the fact that it took me so long to share the story with her, but it still came in bits and pieces. She helped me tremendously once I allowed myself to fully trust her with the demons I had stored away.

The bottle was still secure, and I was slowly working through my problems…then COVID hit. I had COVID for over three weeks. I was quite ill. I was hospitalized overnight, but the worst part was the loneliness. I remember my friend, Charlotte, dropping by…she stood outside and put her hand on the window. I put mine up to hers and broke down crying.

I'm not sure, but I believe COVID triggered the memory that would blow my world apart once again. I'm not sure why it happens, but apparently, it's common for the mind to hide a memory that may prove to be too painful to remember.

The memory seemed to come like a bolt of lightning. I had a memory of another abuse. I can't go into to detail, because innocent people in my life would be hurt as they, too, had been abused by this person and are not ready to share their story. It's not necessary to include details, as it is what happened after the memory that I must share.

Let me begin again…I had a memory come back like a flash of lightning. Once again, I had been abused. The culmination of everything caused the bubbles in the champagne bottle, which held my childhood suffering, to not only send the cork flying but the bottle itself exploded. Suddenly, I was writhing in pain. I felt like I was suffocating. I will equate it to being in the womb, contractions were occurring, but the umbilical cord was around my neck. I was dying. If I didn't get help, I would not survive.

I called my sister weeping. All I could say over and over to her was, "Why did God put me on this earth?" "Why am I here?" She didn't know what to say other than, "You're here for me, Penny."

I sat on my kitchen floor drinking tequila and praying. I wanted to understand why God had placed me on this planet. I could barely breathe. I called my therapist and told her I needed help. I wasn't going to survive. She helped me get to a place in Arizona for an in-house treatment. This place was well known and had a wonderful reputation; however, I was so afraid. I was afraid to face my demons, I was afraid to share my story with other women, but more than anything I was terrified it would not work. What if I didn't find the help I needed. I believed I might be beyond help. What if I left the same?

CHAPTER NINE

On the flight from Nashville to Phoenix, I felt a plethora of emotions. I felt scared, lonely, sick, and yes…excited and hopeful. Not knowing what this would entail, I knew this was an opportunity to rid myself of the demons that I lived with daily and had lived with for most of my life. I knew this opportunity was a gift that I would take full advantage of regardless of my fears. For the first time in my life, I knew I needed help and I believed this might be what I needed to live a life "free." The truth is I had no idea what "free" looked like, and the very idea of it intimidated me to say the least.

When I arrived at my hotel, where I would be staying that night, I went to my room. I felt like a lost little girl. I didn't know what to feel. I didn't know what to think about the next morning when I would be picked up and taken to "Willow House" at the Meadows. That's the name of the house I would be sharing for the next month with nine other women. I would not only be sharing the house, but I would be sharing my life…my truth with them. Seeing as I am a private person and never had many girlfriends, I wasn't sure how I would be able to get over this hurdle. But one thing was certain; I was going to give it all I had. I would do whatever they asked if it meant I would get over the gut-wrenching pain I was enduring.

The next morning came with my having little sleep that night. I would be picked up by someone from the house. I was quite nervous; however, the gentleman who picked me up was so kind. He made me feel completely at ease and safe from the moment I met him. I sat in the back seat of the luxury car he was driving. We didn't speak all that much during the two-hour drive, but when we did, he simply encouraged me. He said in a month, there would be a difference in my life and outlook. I could only respond with, "I hope so."

Upon arriving at the house, the first impression was unimpressive. It was nothing like I had expected. I thought it would have more of a hotel/spa feel, but it was nothing like that in the least. It was a small simple house surrounded by cactus and desert plants. It was quite hot as well, but having come from Nashville with high humidity, this didn't feel all that bad. It was almost comforting. I walked into the house hearing a lot of chatter and laughter. The ladies were all sitting eating lunch together. I felt very intimidated and nervous and didn't really want to look at them; although, I did. I was checked into the house. The tech took my suitcase, which she would be going through to ensure I didn't bring anything that was unacceptable. She took my phone, watch, and headset. I would not be able to make a call for a week, and then it would be supervised on a landline. I was given the layout of the place and a schedule. I was not expected to attend everything that day. I was told I could get my bearings. I was introduced to everyone and had a small bite to eat, then I went outside and went for a walk. I walked several laps. I was told by one of the girls later that she felt my energy and knew this was going to be hard for me.

I was sharing a room with three other ladies, which didn't appeal to me at all…I wanted my own room with privacy. I didn't realize how important it would be for my healing to share not only my story with these women, but it was equally if not more so, important for me to share my life with them. This meant that I would need to live openly with them daily. The whole concept of this house was centered around interaction. As intimidating as this idea was to me, I knew I had to do whatever they requested of me…I needed help!!

I had several meetings set up for that day. I met with the psychiatrist, the nurse, and the medical doctor. I was given an online questionnaire to fill out before I would see the psychologist. The questionnaire took four hours over two days to complete. It asked every possible question imaginable. It wasn't easy, especially for someone who showed up completely raw with emotion. When I finished the test, I laughed at the thought, *Maybe this test is simply to make me feel better once I realized I was done.*

I attended a group therapy session that afternoon. I was told I didn't have to; however, I didn't want to miss any opportunity to start the healing process. I was told should I become uncomfortable or "triggered" in any way I could leave…which I did. I don't recall exactly what prompted me to leave the room, but I had been triggered emotionally.

The schedule for the week would consist of daily group therapy sessions, private therapy sessions, and self-guided therapy. We would also be attending a weekly self-defense class, yoga, tai chi, art therapy, horse therapy, and an obstacle course challenge. We had occasional pool time, and meals throughout the day. My weight would be monitored daily along with food intake. I was given five books to read, which I began immediately. We were encouraged to get to know one another; however, if our boundaries were crossed, we were free to share this with the individual. Speaking up for ourselves was important…this was about our healing process.

After a few days I met with the psychologist. She was supposed to give me a diagnosis based on my answers to the questionnaire I had completed upon arriving. I went into this meeting feeling nervous. "What would she say about me?" To my surprise she stated she didn't know how to diagnose me. Given my history, nothing seemed to match the way I responded to the questions…the way I carried out my life. You would think this would make me feel better; however, it only caused me to feel very insecure. "If they can't diagnose me, how can they treat me?" In the end, I was diagnosed with PTSD and love avoidance syndrome. "What?" I was very familiar with PTSD (Post Traumatic Stress Disorder). I knew a lot of military-members suffered from this; however, it had not occurred to me that I could be suffering from it, and what was "love avoidance?" I had never heard of this term. I was given a book on "love avoidance" to help me understand and work toward recovery. Truthfully, I was thankful to have a diagnosis, simply so I could begin the process of healing.

I didn't offer anything up at first to the group sessions…I simply listened. By listening, I realized these ladies were as broken as I was, and I gradually felt safe. It was an environment of absolutely no judgment with the concentration on healing and supporting one another. I began to relax and trust these ladies. They proved to be the biggest part of my healing process. I will forever be grateful for each of them and the courage it took for them to be vulnerable. I couldn't have done it without them and their attitude of openness about their battles. Not all were like mine, but the level of vulnerability it took to share their story was equal with mine.

It seemed that my toe in the water of my therapy quickly became a full-on immersion into the deep. I had my first one-on-one with my therapist, which proved to be a tough first meeting. I was asked questions regarding my life and abuse. This was simply an overview; however, given the sheer level of raw emotions that I was dealing with, it was one of the hardest meetings I had to endure. There were a few things I wasn't ready to go into detail about, but my therapist was completely understanding and allowed me to take baby steps. The rest of the meetings were based on specific events. I had to face the events and the people in my life. Some were easier than others. Some were heartbreaking. Confronting my faith and the church I grew up in, as well as the perpetrators was difficult; however, the hardest was confronting my mother.

As part of my homework, I had to write a letter to my mom (one she would never read) telling her exactly how I felt. I was told not to hold anything back regarding my feelings. My therapist said this was important because it allowed me to release the feelings I had stored in my body. The letter was longer than I expected it to be, and it also consisted of feelings I didn't know I was carrying. I had blamed my mother for everything. I must be honest here…I didn't realize until I wrote the letter, I absolutely blamed her for everything that had happened to me. After reading it to my therapist at our next meeting, I sat there. I looked at my therapist and said, "I know I should probably want to cry, but I don't think I will." She said that was fine. My feelings were my feelings. However, as I sat there allowing what I had written and what I had been feeling all these years sink in…I broke down. I cried a sobbing cry for a solid thirty-plus minutes. I had placed the guilt of my perpetrators on my mother. I had completely misplaced the guilt and anger on her. It wasn't her fault what had happened to me. The guilt lay with the ones who chose to hurt me.

My mind went to all the times my mother asked me to forgive her and believing I had, I would tell her, "Mom, I do forgive you. Please let's not talk about this anymore." I denied my mother the only thing she wanted from me while she was alive…my forgiveness. This was difficult for me to face, but it was something I needed to release. I only wish I could have allowed her to receive the forgiveness during her life. Having said that, I also realize I couldn't do that without the treatment I was now receiving. I had to face my feelings before I could ever give anything more to her. It's regrettable, but it couldn't be helped. I gave what I could give. I love my mother. I have loved her my whole life and I am grateful we were able to achieve a relationship of love before she passed away, but that was the most I could give her at the time.

I'm so grateful God not only gave her grace, but he also showed me grace by allowing me to fully forgive her for the things that deserved forgiveness. Mom should never have been held accountable for the abuse I endured, therefore, forgiveness was not something that she should have to receive. I've learned through this process; it is so easy to misplace the blame. It, in a way, helps us as the victims to blame those around us who are accessible to us, since our abusers usually are not. I will forever be grateful I understand my mother was not at fault for the evil intent of my perpetrators.

Let's move on…. During art therapy I was asked to make a poster using photos, drawings, and words to describe my abuse as I saw it. My poster included many things, but the one thing I had to face was my church and my faith in that denomination. Let me reiterate…I didn't lose my faith in God…but I had to confront the fact that I not only blamed my mother, but I also blamed my church. Afterall, my abuse had almost entirely been inflicted by the men who were of the same faith.

I left the center of my poster empty. I stared at it. I noticed several of the ladies, but especially one who watched me, then I finally mustered up the courage to face the truth of my pain. I placed a cross in the center of the poster. I wrote the words…not God…my church. I had to face the fact that I believed the church had not only been the source of my faith and belief in God, but it was also the source of my pain. I remember one of the girls said, "I wondered if you would put that in there." She knew I was struggling with this idea, but in the end, it was something I had to do. She told me she was proud of me as did some of the other ladies. A few were surprised, but knew it was something I needed to face.

My therapy was made complete through the obstacle challenges and horse therapy. One of the obstacles required me to climb to the top of a power pole and leap from it to hit a ball that dangled slightly higher than the pole and approximately three feet from the pole. I had nothing to hang on to, but I was harnessed to safety lines. I had to trust the ones, holding the lines, would catch me and not let me fall. I stood on top of the pole, looked down at the ladies below. They were yelling at me, "You've got this, Penny!" I leaped and hit the ball. I felt the cables tighten and slowly lower me to the ground. Another obstacle required me to work with another girl to climb to the top of several poles tethered together. This obstacle absolutely required that we trust and help one another to reach the top. I have no doubt you understand the purpose of this obstacle. I had to learn to trust other people to help me in life. I had to trust that there were people who could be trusted and wanted me to survive, but more than survival… there were people who wanted me to live the best life possible.

The horse therapy opened my eyes to my own grief and emotions. I didn't know it until my last week in horse therapy; however, the horse I gravitated to, which was often alone, had been a rescue from an abusive situation. He was the only horse I wanted to be with, although we were encouraged to be with other horses. He was the one I sought out to be with every week.

Interestingly, I realized every decision I made in my life was influenced by my abuse. Through acknowledging these events, I was able to put them in a place where I could accept them, but not allow them to control my life.

Through prayer, tai chi, yoga, meditation, realizing my boundaries, and of course self-defense, I learned that my mind, body, and spirit are all connected, and each has equal importance in keeping me on the right path, and it is my duty to care for each of these. I had to learn to realize my boundaries and not allow anyone to cross them. I had to learn to give myself grace for the things I couldn't change and the mistakes I felt I had made along my path.

There are so many things I could share with you about this month of therapy—for instance: reading my books, walking daily chatting with these beautiful women, and going to the meditation room whenever it was available to me—but my favorite was getting up around four every morning to watch the sunrise. I never missed it. Watching the sun come up over the desert mountains, watching the cactus flowers come to life, and feeling the cool temperatures, which were so opposite of the hot day that was approaching…it set the tone for my healing, because the desert seemed to teach me each morning about new beginnings. It reminded me that even in the desert, where seemingly out of rock and sand, a beautiful flower emerges, and because I didn't have a phone or camera, I lived in the moment. I completely internalized what I was seeing and feeling. I'm so grateful for this experience because it has helped me to live in the present. Not to simply take photos, but to feel, hear, and enjoy what is going on around me.

I learned many important things through my treatment. I learned that I am not alone in the world, and I am valuable. I learned it's OK to trust people. I learned that I am not guilty of the things that happened to me…I realized this as I listened to the women who were there sharing the stories of their lives. I knew they were not at fault and eventually I started realizing I wasn't either. Over the next several weeks, years of doubt, shame, and insecurity fell from my body. I no longer carried that burden. I was no longer living in the womb. I had been reborn. I was innocent, and I was free to start my life anew. I was excited, but not fully aware of the challenge that I faced once I left the Willow House.

PART THREE

CHAPTER TEN

I'm always amazed at how many emotions a person can feel seemingly at the same time. I arrived at the Willow House with a "plethora" of emotions. Now, I was leaving the Willow House with a "plethora" of emotions. They were similar, yet quite different. I was anxious and excited to be in a place where my healing could begin, and now…I was so excited about the newness of how I felt when I got into the backseat of the same luxury sedan, with the same driver, who had picked me up over a month ago to take me to the Willow House.

A few days prior to leaving, I had made a reservation at a spa resort in Phoenix. I thought it would be a good place to allow what I had experienced to sink in before heading home. I was excited about having a nice dinner that evening. I was looking forward to sitting by the pool, relaxing in the spa, while enjoying this newfound freedom that came through having taken off my armor. This would be the perfect beginning to my new life.

As we pulled up to the resort, I felt butterflies of excitement. I was starting over…I was reborn. This feeling lasted right up to the point my driver pulled away. I would like to share with you that as I write this, I can feel the butterflies in my stomach turning to anxiety. This is the same feeling I had when my driver left me standing there on the sidewalk at the entrance of the resort check-in. I didn't hear the bellman ask to show me to the counter. My armor was gone, and I felt fully exposed. I felt completely alone and vulnerable.

After checking in, I was taken to my beautiful suite, which included a view of the mountains. The front desk had upgraded me… it was as if they could see that I needed a little extra care. Although grateful, it made me feel even more exposed. Any other situation, I would have been so excited about my room and the few days I would be spending here, but I was like a child.

Unsure of why I was feeling this way, I called the nurse at the Willow House. She told me this was a normal reaction. She instructed me to take my anxiety medication as needed; however, she felt I should take them for the next week as directed by daily dosage. She made sure I knew she was a phone call away should I have any questions. She encouraged me, which gave me the confidence to go to dinner.

I arrived at the restaurant excited about the meal…I'm quite the foodie. The table where I sat was next to the massive window that went from floor to ceiling and wall to wall. The view was nothing short of spectacular, with it being the mountains displayed in pinks and orange due to the sunset. I looked at it and felt small and vulnerable once again. I was so uncomfortable, I had to have the waiter wrap my meal to go. I went back to the room, put on a robe, and sat outside on the terrace eating my meal, the little I could get down. I ended up going to the living room, lying down on the floor, and started a meditation video from YouTube. I didn't watch it. I simply closed my eyes and listened. I turned on the TV afterwards, but quickly turned it off; it was all too much for me to handle. It's hard to explain, but it was intense to the point I am having a difficult time writing about it. My emotions were so raw. I was so new to this life. I was trying to navigate it but quickly realized it was a lot to face alone. What I realized later is that I was never alone. God was with me. He was with me spiritually, but he was also with me through my family, friends, and caregivers; however, at this moment…I felt alone.

I eventually took my medication and went to bed. The next morning, I had breakfast delivered to my room. Again, I sat on the terrace enjoying my coffee and the view. I also enjoyed being alone not having to speak with anyone. I was safe with me; however, I knew this was not healthy, so I dressed and mustered up the courage to walk around the resort. I ended up in the spa where I scheduled my massage, facial, manicure and pedicure, which I would enjoy over the next several days.

My massage was scheduled for that afternoon. I arrived early and sat in the relaxation room. I had a cup of hot tea and contemplated my future. It was a bit to take in, so I tried to focus on relaxing, while enjoying this beautiful, relaxing room. My massage was such a wonderful surprise of peace and relaxation. I was slowly feeling like I would be able to move within this new life that was now mine.

After my massage, I went to the room, changed into my swimsuit, grabbed a book and headed to the pool. I felt so relaxed; however, this was short-lived.

As I sat by the pool, a man and his daughter, who were a few chairs over, started talking to me. When they asked what brought me to Arizona, I was immediately taken back. *What do I tell them…what am I supposed to say?* Although their question was completely innocent and one that anyone would consider simply being social, it made me feel exposed. Once again, I wanted to go to the room and hide, but I stayed and tried to get lost in my book; however, I was fully aware of everyone around me. A man came and sat next to me, and all I could do was pray in my head that he would not talk to me. We did speak briefly. He had a very calming presence, so I was able to enjoy my time reading. I eventually got in the pool. I enjoyed it right up until someone approached me. I didn't want to speak to him, but I smiled, said a few things, and left as soon as I could. I just wanted to go back to my room.

When I got back to the room, I put my robe on and was about to order my dinner when I received a call from the Willow House. The nurse informed me the doctor had ordered some medication for me. I could pick it up at the Walgreens not far from where I was staying. I decided I would Uber and pick it up before ordering dinner.

I sat outside the entrance to the check-in counter at the resort waiting on the Uber that would take me to pick up my medication and then return me to the property. When the Uber arrived, I got in the car completely unprepared for the emotion I was going to feel as we pulled away. The driver was nice enough; however, he was complaining about a few mindless things, but it was this mindless conversation in the confined space that caused me to panic. I covered it up, but I was completely panicked in the backseat. I put my hand on the door handle engaging all the strength I had to keep from opening the door of this moving car and jumping out. I felt like I would vomit as I tried to hide that I was hyperventilating. When we arrived at Walgreens, I told him I had decided to shop a bit and would not need him to take me back to the resort. The truth is that I needed time to breathe. I took my anxiety medication and walked around a bit before getting my prescription. Once I felt calm, I ordered another Uber.

Upon arriving at my room, I put my robe on, sat on the terrace, and waited for the dinner I had ordered to arrive. Once it arrived, I returned to the terrace to eat. As I ate, I watched the mountains change colors, then took in the sky as it was taken over by millions of stars. I felt small yet special as I thought of the vastness of the universe and the fact that God had placed me here in this moment of healing to see the beauty, he had created… and at that moment, I believed he had done it for me.

The next day arrived, and I awoke to the breakfast I had ordered the night before. After I ate, I went to the living room, prayed, and meditated. Afterwards, I headed to the spa to enjoy the amenities before my next treatment. I then went to the pool and read my book. I avoided having to talk to anyone but felt a little more at ease when I did. I ate all my dinners in the room, while enjoying the sunsets. I thought about all the sunrises I had enjoyed and now the sunsets. I felt the sunrises had ushered in my new freedom, and now the sunsets were closing the door on the past. I was starting over. I was nowhere near comfortable in my skin…I had a lot of learning to do in this new body I now lived in, and it would not come without pitfalls…it would not come without trying to put the old armor back on…it would not come without moments that seemed like failure… but it also would not come without victories. I was on my way to learning to walk again, but I had to learn to talk again, I had to learn to trust again, and I had to get to know the real Penny…her strength, her weaknesses, and her beauty as a creation of God, while also having to learn to trust him again.

CHAPTER ELEVEN

I must tell you how difficult this is for me to write; although, I believe it is the most important part. I was reborn, but I had not learned to navigate in this new body of mine. I was making bad decision after bad decision. I had a friend comment that they thought I was through with this, but what they did not understand was I had to face life without my armor, and I basically was learning to live again. I had to accept my vulnerability, which meant that I had to trust myself and others with "Penny" …the real Penny. I was facing rejection as I am. If I was rejected before, I could deal with it because I had the armor of protection around me…the armor that basically said, "Rejection is inevitable because of what you've been through." Now that I no longer carried that safety net with me, I would face rejection of me, and I was still trying to get to know me as well. It other words, I was trying to learn my strengths…my weaknesses…my dreams, and most importantly…my faith.

I'm not going to go into depth about all the times I stumbled, but there were many. I guess I feel it's important for you to know that you're not alone if you slip. I don't know how many times I tried to put my armor back on but knew the life I now lived out of the womb and in the light was so much better and more rewarding than the life I had confined in a womb of my own creation.

I want you to remember…It's not a failure if you slip and fall. It's simply a learning moment. Every time I slipped, I learned from it. I grew. However, with all that was going on in my life…my faith still needed work. Of course, I had not given up on God, but my eyes were not on him. Remember I told you that God never failed to provide what I needed at any given time. Well, this was not different. I not only had my family, but God sent random people into my life to remind me to focus my eyes on God.

I was in a restaurant sitting at the bar eating. I was writing in my journal. I was having a bad night. I spoke briefly to the couple beside me. I left and went to the bathroom, packed up and went home. I didn't pick up my journal for quite some time, but when I did, the following was written in my book…

> *"Dear Ms. Penny,*
> *It was a pleasure meeting you. I want you to know you have a wonderful soul. You have an ability to help people in a way no one else can. Keep your eyes on God. He has a plan for your life. I will be praying for you.*
> *God Bless You!"*

I want you to know my faith was always in God, the problem was that I had not given it to him. I had not given him my fears. I had not trusted him to be my parent and allow him to protect me as I learned to navigate this life I was now living. But that did not change the fact that he continued to bring reminders of his love for me.

My family not only made it clear they were there to love me, but they were also there to be sure I didn't go down the wrong path. When they did suspect life was getting to be overwhelming, they confronted me. I am so grateful. I know it wasn't easy for them to confront me, but I am so grateful to be loved that much. It's not been easy for me to accept help, but that's a part of my healing. It needs to be a part of your healing. Accepting help needs to be a part of your life. I wouldn't be where I am without my family and friends who encouraged me. The ones who said, "We like this Penny."

As I slowly began to trust myself, I made some changes in my life. I left Facebook for starters. I then decided to move out of my apartment in Brentwood. My plan was to store all my belongings, move between staying with my family and Airbnbs for a year until I knew exactly what I wanted to do. This would allow me to travel, read, and write. I felt encouraged to write my story. I also had my doubts…but God never failed to give the encouragement I needed. You see, one of the changes I made in my life was to start listening to inspirational speeches. One morning I listened to Denzel Washington. Feeling insecure about sharing my life, I listened to him say… "Put God First…Don't be afraid to fail Big." After I listened to him, I got up from my chair outside, made my bed, and committed to praying and studying my Bible every morning before I began my day. I was already reading a scripture every night before I went to sleep, but I knew I needed more.

Since committing to this, I noticed changes in myself. I no longer felt insecure. Do I have insecure moments…absolutely! I voiced an observation to my sister, "It's funny how God has brought these new, quality people into my life as I am preparing to move."

She commented, "It is something to think about." Then she went on to say, "Why do you think that is? What is different about you today from six months ago?"

I said, "I'm happy with me, and I'm living a better quality of life."

She said, "That's right!" She had the attitude of, "I told you so"; although, she never said that to me.

I want you to know my life is not without setbacks, but I have learned to have faith in the goodness of people. I've learned to speak with confidence as the person I am now, without the shame of what I've been through. I continue to develop my walking skills as I still stumble; however, I realize if I keep my eyes on God's promises and love for me, I'm able to keep going with the full knowledge that although I may stumble as I continue this journey of walking again, I know I am not alone. God is always with me…my family is with me, and because I have allowed people into my life…my friends are there as well. I know this will be an ongoing learning experience, since I have only just begun to get to know me…the real Penny, but it's one filled with color, newness, true friendship, true relationships, true joy, but mostly Truth…I no longer live in a lie. I have been freed from the lie that I'm not good enough as I am, I don't deserve happiness, and that I don't deserve love. Because the truth is I am good enough, I do deserve happiness, and I do deserve love!

CHAPTER TWELVE

Before closing, I would like to briefly share with you how I came to choose "Learning to Walk Again" as the title of my story. Not only the title but the writing of the entire book, was inspired by the words of the song, "Walk" by the Foo Fighters. I was in my kitchen cooking or cleaning…I'm not sure which, but I do know I was dancing to random music that popped-up on YouTube. "Walk" came on and as I was dancing and listening to the song, I stopped. I thought…this is my life, this is what I have gone through, this is where I am! I hadn't thought lately about writing a book; although, I had in the past. I wrote one twenty years ago, but it was all for me. But this was different because my story was now complete. I had learned to "Walk Again." It was dancing in my kitchen where I knew I had to write my story and I knew what I needed to write…

Penny McIntyre-Crain

"Walk"
"A million miles away
Your signal in the distance
To whom it may concern

I think I lost my way
Getting good at starting over
Every time that I return

Learning to walk again
I believe I've waited long enough
Where do I begin?

Learning to talk again
Can't you see I've waited long enough?
Where do I begin?

Do you remember the days?
We built these paper mountains
Then sat and watched them burn

I think I found my place
Can't you feel it growing stronger
Little conquerors

. . .

Now

Learning to Walk Again

For the very first time
Don't you pay no mind
Set me free, again

To keep alive, a moment at a time
That's still inside, a whisper to a riot
The sacrifice, the knowing to survive
The first decline, another state of mind

I'm on my knees, I'm praying for a sign
Forever, whenever, I never wanna die

. . .

I'm dancing on my grave
I'm running through the fire
Forever, whenever
I never wanna die

I never wanna leave
I'll never say goodbye
Forever, whenever
Forever, whenever

Learning to walk again
I believe I've waited long enough
Where do I begin?

Learning to walk again
I believe I've waited long enough
Learning to talk again
Can't you see I've waited long enough?!"

I had been lost and pretended to be OK. I did want to die. It had been approximately forty years since my initial abuse, and I had lived all these years with my bottled-up, messy life. I had allowed it to dictate my life choices and my responses to situations. I had allowed it also to be a hiding place. I used my "armor" to hide "Penny." There are so many sad aspects of this truth, but one of the saddest is I didn't allow people to accept me as I am. I didn't give anyone a chance to see the real me. I didn't give myself the opportunity to see me either… the one who loves to sing, the one who loves to dance, the one who loves life and desperately wants to enjoy every second of everyday. I allowed lies, pain, and anger to be my strength. I never truly gave peace, joy, and love a chance to be my armor. What I have discovered is these three things protect me in a way that the armor I had created for myself never could; because I am able to move, laugh, experience life in a way I never had before…in a way I didn't know was possible. I had waited long enough to receive the care I needed.

God could not show me my true value until I took off my armor, so he could reveal the true Penny…the one he created. I envision this as looking at myself in the mirror, while God dictated to those who helped me along the way to remove pieces of the armor I wore. As each piece was removed, it revealed wounds that couldn't heal because they never received the proper attention required to heal. I was horrified to look at them. I felt ugly and grotesque as I stood there naked, covered in wounds. I wanted to put the armor back on; however, the ones who were around me began to apply medicine. They encouraged me while turning me from the mirror. They directed my eyes toward God. I wept at my humanity as I still tried to cover my body, then God directed my caregivers to wash my face, cleanse my body, and place a robe on me. Then he instructed me to look in the mirror again. I didn't want to, but with my eyes tightly closed, he slowly turned me around and said, "Child, see what I see." I carefully and slowly opened my eyes. I was beautifully scarred. I appeared to be glowing. I had a beauty that radiated from the inside out through each scar. I smiled as I realized I was worthy to be loved.

My life is far from perfect; however, each day brings an immeasurable amount of hope and excitement about my future. Having said that, I realize my future is now and today is the day the Lord has given me, and I will laugh. I will sing. I will dance. But mostly I will experience, fully, the joy God has given me through my scars, though my healing, through his Love.

I pray you find your way to "Walking Again." It's a difficult journey, but you are worth it!!! You are worthy of Hope, Joy, and especially Love!!!

God Bless You!
Penny